REFLECTIONS

POEMS OF
LIFE AND LOVE

KATHRYN CAROLE ELLISON

Published by Lady Bug Books, an imprint of Brisance Books Group.
Lady Bug Press and the distinctive ladybug logo are registered trademarks of
Lady Bug Books, LLC.

Lady Bug Books
400 112th Avenue N.E.
Suite 230
Bellevue, WA 98004
www.GiftsOfLove.com

For information about custom editions, special sales and permissions, please email
Info@GiftsOfLove.com

Manufactured in the United States of America
ISBN: 978-1-944194-83-3

First Edition: November 2021

A NOTE FROM THE AUTHOR

The poems in this book were written over many years as gifts to my children. I began writing them in the 1970s, when they were reaching the age of reason. And, as I found myself in the position of becoming a single parent, I wanted to do something special to share with them – something that would become a tradition, a ritual they could count on.

And so the Advent Poems began – one day, decades ago – with a poem 'gifted' to them each day during the Advent period leading up to Christmas, December 1 to December 24. Forty some years later… my children still look forward each year to the poems that started a family tradition, that new generations have come to cherish.

It is my sincere hope that you will embrace and enjoy them, and share them with those you love.

Children of the Light was among the early poems I wrote, and is included in each of the *Poems of Life and Love* books in The Ellison Collection: *Heartstrings, Celebrations, Inspirations, Sanctuary, Awakenings, Sojourns, Milestones, Tapestry, Gratitude, Beginnings, Horizons, Moments, Possibilities, Mindfulness and Reflections.* After writing many hundreds of poems, it is still my favorite. The words came from my heart… and my soul… and flowed so effortlessly that it was written in a single sitting.
All I needed to do was capture the words on paper.

Light, to me, represented all that was good and pure and right with the world, and I believed then – as I do today – that those elements live in my children, and perhaps in all of us. We need only to dare.

– KCE

Dedication

To my parents: Herb and Bernice Haas

Mom, you were the poet who went before me...
unpublished, but appreciated nonetheless.

And Dad, you always believed in me,
no matter what direction my life took.
Thank you for your faith in me,
and for your unconditional love.

TABLE OF CONTENTS

LIFE'S JOYS

LIFE'S LESSONS

LIFE'S GIFTS

LIFE'S JOYS

TRUTH

The truth is not open to question; incontrovertible.
Malice and ignorance may attack or deride.
But in the end, when the confusion is laid to rest,
There it is – in the open – not to be denied.

Truth is, by its nature, self-evident,
And will always be the ultimate power.
It can be glossed over, and otherwise contradicted,
But will not go away. Truth does not cower.

The great enemy of the truth is often not the lie,
But it's the myth persuasive and persistent.
John F. Kennedy shared this wisdom some time ago.
There's no doubt about what his words meant.

It is not because the truth is too difficult to see
That mistakes are made in the process.
It's because our most comfortable course of action
Is one that accords with our own selfish interest.

Mahatma Gandhi said, "Morality is the basis of things,
And truth is the substance of all morality."
Truth will always be truth, whether understood or not.
There's only one truth; there is no duality.

"Whoever is careless with the truth in small matters,"
According to Einstein near the end of his days,
"Cannot be trusted with the important ones."
The pattern is set early and is lived out in most ways.

THE POWER OF THOUGHTS

Imagine a flower in a pot
Or a sculpture you'll carve in soap...
Imagine an encounter with someone you love,
Or a goal upon which you've placed hope...

Thoughts and imaginings are powerful.
They're the first step to attain any object.
The bridge, or the garden, was first a dream
Before it became a project.

No matter how large or small a thing
The human mind does conjure,
It's first an idea. Then follows the plan,
And work to manufacture.

The difference between a thought
And a physical reality
Is a certain amount of time and, too,
An amount of physical activity.

DIVINE

The spark within that resonates
With the loving God who celebrates
The pairing of our soul with Hers/His
Is our connection to the "all that is."

We were born with a body this time around.
It made us human to be earth-bound.
But God added a spark that lives deep within.
It's our soul that connects us to our origin.

This spark of the divine, or soul, we hold
Is worthy of the same respect, I am told,
That is given to God when we go to prayer.
It's our connection to Him/Her — another layer.

SIMPLICITY

Thoreau and many others wrote about simplicity...
The message "Keep it simple" is everywhere.
It's an art worth practicing, simplifying one's life,
But a trait, among most humans, very rare.

The art of simplicity is simply to simplify!
(Truly much easier said than done)
It is the mark of greatness... "To be simple is to be great,"
Wrote Emerson in paradoxical fun.

Simplicity avoids the superficial;
No winding detours off the beaten path.
It's the shortest distance between two points.
It's language can even be math.

Simplicity emphasizes the obvious to us all.
It does not elucidate the veiled.
It works as a tool to solve our problems,
When other methods have failed.

Simplicity has given all the big things we treasure
Little names for more comprehension.
"Dawn," "day," "hope" and "love;" "home," "peace,"
"life" and "death"
Have meanings too numerous to mention.

Simplicity deepens life; it magnifies the virtues,
Without which man wouldn't survive.
The questions decrease as the knowledge sinks in.
It's a step to feeling alive.

Simplicity is the arrow of the spirit, it's said.
It can be eloquent, or a muttered aside.
It's the most direct way I know of to truth,
And a lot more comfortable ride.

MANY WAYS TO SHOW LOVE

There are many ways to show one's love.
The trick can be to finding the key.
Your patience and kindness and caring ways
Result in letting people be
Just who they are, without your expectations.
Do not judge their actions or deeds.
It must be understood quite thoroughly
That people are acting out of THEIR needs.

Your friendship will be sought by others if you
Provide a safe, loving space for them to be
Just who they are without the need
Of having to prove they're okay.

JOGGING

Jogging is supposed to be good for the heart –
It's supposed to make your lungs cry!
It strengthens muscles and makes juices flow,
Producing a euphoric high!

However, the look of anguish and despair
That contorts jogger's faces when they run,
Huffing and puffing by the side of the road,
Makes jogging look like not very much fun!

HOME

It's a funny thing when you return back home,
After being away on your own for awhile.
Everything looks and feels, and even smells, the same.
You see familiar things, and you smile.

There's a longing to return, just for a moment,
To the former life you led back then
Where you knew things for sure – they were cut and dried.
You wonder about the way things might have been.

But you went away, to school, to work, to life.
You learned things 'they' didn't know.
It's hard to find common ground for conversation,
So you listen... with some wonder and some sorrow.

Now that you're grown and have your own life,
You realize you now must find your own way.
You establish your home and circle of friends,
And your childhood is a memory... a far distance away.

"Home" for you is not a place, it's a feeling.
Home is where you hang your heart.
Home is people, your family and friends...
A feeling you carry inside, if you're smart.

BEAUTY

It's said that true beauty comes from within,
A statement I agree with, it's true!
But features and bone structure add to the mix
To enhance what is found within you.

Be grateful for features that God saw fit
To bestow upon you at birth.
Let them work for you, for they reflect
How you express your own self-worth.

It's a cycle, because when you feel good
About yourself, it really shows.
And seeing that beauty and owning it
Fosters the process, and then it grows.

First impressions are important; they well may be
Your one chance to make your thoughts known.
And how you appear when you present your cause
Can encourage that interest to be shown.

Remember the movie about the 'Force?'
'May the Force be with you,' Obi said.
That Force brings confidence and with it you can
Create reality from the pictures in your head.

HAPPINESS

"Most folks are as happy as they make up their minds to be."
– Abe Lincoln

Happiness is sought all over the world.
Everyone wants happiness in their lives every day.
True happiness is to enjoy the present, without anxiety
About the future along the way.

The Constitution gives people the right to pursue happiness.
But you, yourself, have to make it your own.
Happiness is the absence of striving for it.
You are responsible for it; yes, you alone.

You must try to generate happiness within yourself;
It does not come to you from the outside.
Happiness is a direction, not a place or a thing.
And when it comes to you... relax, and let it reside.

Be happy for this and every moment!
It's your life, after all, and you are in command!
Happiness comes to you through your own actions.
You must share it to enjoy it, you understand.

Happiness does not depend on what you have...
It does not come to you from afar.
Happiness is found in doing, not possessing.
So, your happiness depends on what you are.

GRATITUDE

Giving with love and accepting with gratitude
Is the foundation for all abundance.
If you're not thankful for all that you have
You probably won't like what is coming (perchance).

The best way to take away the pain from the past
Is to replace the hurt with gratitude.
Gratitude can transform any situation.
It requires only a change of attitude.

When you count your blessings, your life turns for the better.
Nothing is more attractive than a grateful heart.
Gratitude is the gateway to a positive life.
There's no room for negativity, right from the start.

The more grateful you are, the more beauty you see.
Gratitude unlocks the fullness of life,
And it shifts you to a higher frequency
Where fear disappears, and also any strife.

You are more alive being aware of your treasures.
Being thankful for what you have will bring you more!
A grateful heart is a magnet for miracles!
You have an invitation to a happier life, therefore.

CHILDREN OF THE LIGHT

There are those souls who bring the light,
Who spill it out for all to share.
And with a joy that does excite,
They show the world that they do care.
It is so very bright.

In this sharing, love does pervade
Into their lives and cycles round;
And as this light is outward played
The love is also inward bound.
It is an awesome trade.

You are a soul whose light is shared.
It comes from deep within your heart.
It's best because it is not spared,
Because it's total, not just part.
And I am glad you've dared.

GOODNESS

Goodness is mostly about character:
Integrity, Honesty, and Kindness for sure;
With Moral Courage and Generosity thrown in,
Along with added Love, for good measure.
But more than anything else it's how you treat
Other people. That is your signature.

Treat those who are good with goodness;
And treat those who are not, the same.
Sometimes it becomes a challenge,
But Goodness is the name of the game.
In the end you stay true to your nature.
Goodness is attained. That's the aim.

It's said that the fragrance of the flowers
Spreads only in the direction of the breeze.
This diffusion of fragrance is dependent
On an outside source, if you please,
While the Goodness of a person is spread
In all directions, sweet-scented, and with ease.

A FOUR LETTER WORD

If I could have everything I wanted
It would be summed up in a four-letter word.
It would encompass everything in the universe;
Mysteries would be solved; answers delivered.

The word's the thing, or is it a description?
Philosophers have argued over and over.
But one thing is sure; I get to practice
And learn how to really savor
Its meaning, its impact, on my life each day.
And, depending on how centered I am,
I either personify the word, or I do not;
And then I get to practice again.

The word is "love," and from the word
All things good in the world are at hand.
We're brought into each other's lives for a reason:
To experience these four letters firsthand.

LIFE'S LESSONS

BALANCE

Balance is the key, the key to living
A life that is happy and whole...
Balance between your unfolding paths
As you aim onward toward your goal.

First, the physical path, and that's the basis
On which the other paths lie...
Keeping fit, eating right, and resting when tired
Will give you energy to pursue the "why."

And so you move on, your curiosity seeks answers
To the questions in your minds.
Your mental juices are flowing now;
You're open to information of all kinds.

So many people get stuck right here –
They think physical and mental are all.
They may look good and know a few things,
But soon discover a pitfall.

Because, for balance, it takes a third;
And that's faith, or the spiritual source.
That source gives you direction you cannot find
When you study the incomplete course.

The questions will come, they spring eternal.
Curiosity, as the nature of man, is a fact.
But you have the answers, or know how to get them,
If the balance remains intact.

UNCLUTTER YOUR LIFE

Do you ever feel that instead of you owning
Your "stuff," that it owns you?
It clutters your life, it gets in the way
Of living the way you choose.

Clear out the "stuff" no longer useful to you.
There are others who need it, no doubt.
You feel a rush of joy and relief
To have finally thrown it out!!

Donate your "stuff" for others to use.
There are charities just waiting for the goods.
Then sit back and smile at your good luck
To have "uncluttered," in all likelihood.

HONESTY

Honesty is about more than not lying.
It's being truthful in all aspects of your life:
Truth telling, truth speaking, truth living,
And truth loving for a conscience without strife.

Honesty is the fastest way to prevent
A mistake from turning into a failure.
Honesty is something you can't ever wear out.
It has lasting power. It is pure.

The high road is always respected;
Play by your own set of values.
There's no legacy so rich as honesty.
(It's not necessarily learned in school.)

"Honesty is the first chapter
In the Book of Wisdom," it was said.
Thomas Jefferson uttered those words.
(At least to him they were credited.)

EXISTENCE: LIFE AND DEATH

Existence consists of both life and death.
To deny this fact is only moot.
To favor one or the other denies what is,
And causes tension in everyday life, to boot.

Tension causes people to make mistakes
In a sometimes critical situation.
Mistakes are far more deadly than
Existence, and that's no speculation.

It is said that about thirty percent
Of all people love life and fear death.
While yet another thirty percent
Yearn longingly to draw their last breath.

More amazingly still (it's sad but true)
Another thirty percent fear both.
They're afraid to live and afraid to die;
To enjoy their days with grace, they are loathe.

Summed up, that makes ninety percent
Of people who suffer from undue pain.
Their knowledge of how polarities work
Is lost to tension. It's all in vain.

Even though life and death are opposed
They are inseparable, and don't split apart.
Preferences are futile, and a hopeless dance.
(This wisdom is very necessary to impart.)

Only ten percent of the people in the world
Accept both life and death. Meantime,
They simply enjoy the dance of existence,
Knowing growth and decay exist at the same time.

LEADERSHIP

Leadership is about vision and responsibility,
And never about power or fame.
Great leaders don't tell you what to do;
They show how it's done, then you do the same.

True leadership is, basically, about servanthood,
Putting interests (or safety) of others at the center of decisions.
The true test of a leader is how well he does in crisis.
In crises, the actions must be made with precision.

Leaders have the courage to make unpopular choices.
And in leadership, character is more important than strategy.
Leadership is taking the reins in solving problems,
Seeking help from experts along the way.

A leader realizes he's not always the smartest in the room,
And listens, and learns from those who are in the know.
It's not about making speeches, or being liked.
Leadership is defined by results, it would follow.

When leadership is lacking, there is much finger-pointing,
And many arguments about who is to blame.
Leadership is about taking responsibility
With no excuses. The leader must carry the flame.

A leader must do the right thing, even if painful.
He, or She, must do what needs to be done,
With truth and goodness, love and compassion.
The leader should lead others to the best solution.

One more thing, before this poem is finished:
A true leader is humble and can admit his mistakes.
He takes a little more than his share of the blame
And less than his share of credit, for goodness sakes!

TRUTHFULNESS

It's said there are three things
That cannot be hidden for long:
The sun, the moon, and the truth.
They'll appear again, more strong.

Shut up truth, if you will,
Or bury it underground...
Truth will grow again;
It will always be found.

If you don't take truth seriously
In matters that seem small,
Then you cannot be trusted
In large ones, after all.

And if you don't tell the truth
About yourself (it's a bother),
Then you cannot even begin
To tell the truth about another.

Truth needs no rehearsal...
You don't have to play ahead.
It's either true or it isn't.
Enter the conversation without dread.

EXPRESS FEELINGS WITH COURAGE

On the subject of regrets at the end of life
Many people expressed lack of courage
To communicate their feelings, in order to keep peace,
And thus began the damage.

A lifetime of not expressing your feelings
And stifling your reactions to things in your life
Can lead to illness, brought on by resentments
And bitterness carried from a lifetime of strife.

When you change the way you've been by speaking up,
Your friends and family are likely to react.
It will raise your relationships to a more honest level,
Ending the unhealthiness – with your life intact.

FAITH

Faith is such an oddball thing to have;
There's little emotion or fact involved at all.
It is beyond description, but for the feelings
Of peace that set the theme for life overall.

When you have faith there is no need to rule
The actions of your fellow humans, or your own.
The need is gone to guide another's life,
And in its place is harmony, before unknown.

RESPECTING DIFFERENCES

Democracy is not the assumption of leadership
By the few who have won the election;
But is based on the wisdom, the conscience and participation,
Of the many who will shape the direction.

It's the give and take in our society that makes
Our nation strong and viable to the rest.
When everyone thinks alike, nobody thinks!
How we work together and communicate is the test!

Divisiveness and making the other person wrong
For having a point of view that differs
From one we hold is not the way to solve
Any problems. It just makes matters worse.

It's not our differences that divide us. Oh, no!
It is our inability to recognize and accept
That not everyone thinks or believes the same.
Respect for others will win! (What a concept!)

Respect for ourselves guides our morals,
While respect for others guides our manners.
Respecting others' opinions does not necessarily mean
We drop our own, and carry their, banners!

Appreciating the similarities is the first step, I believe,
To communication between opposite opinions;
Then respecting the differences while in discussion,
Giving the relationship the most important attention.

The respect we show to others (or the lack thereof)
Immediately reflects on our own self-respect.
Show respect to people whether they deserve it or not.
It doesn't define their character, but yours it does reflect.

Speak your honest convictions and feelings,
And prepare to live with the consequences.
Remember to appreciate your similarities,
And don't forget to respect the differences!

KARMA

Karma is a subject that is not discussed In most circles.
People become nonplussed.
But how can we know all the things that we do
In one lifetime? Tell me! How about you?

You enter the world, you struggle to grow,
Learning things to add to what you already know.
How did you come by your prior knowledge?
In the womb I don't believe there was a college!

Karma is described as a simple balance –
A balance of experiences marked sometimes with jubilance.
If you were poor in one life, in the next you try rich.
If ugly, then beautiful – you decide which.

A former cripple might come back as an athlete –
You get the picture – you round out to complete
The balance of experience as you look to become whole.
Growth and experience is always your goal.

There is no such thing as bad karma – or good.
You will select what you need, it is understood.
The only judgment comes from yourself and from God.
You balance the inequalities as through lives you plod.

MERCY

All the great concepts are simple.
They can be expressed in a single word:
Freedom, Justice, Honor and Duty;
Hope and Mercy, too, I've heard.

This poem will define the word "Mercy."
Words to define it are numerous.
"Charity, Clemency and Leniency;
Courtesy, Indulgence;" some quite humorous.

Loving one's enemies is difficult,
But imperative for humankind.
Some think compassion and mercy
Can deliver one to his right mind.

As the firmament embraces our world,
Or the sun pours forth its beams,
Mercy must encircle both friend and foe.
It's really much simpler than it seems.

SOME RULES HAVE TO BE BROKEN

Reach out from that still small place,
That taciturn state, that lonely isle.
Stretch forth, smashing old rules
That cling awkwardly to the past.
Be free from the tired old past,
The wearying, worrying approach to life.
Break free from compliance, and breathe!
Get on with your business of living your life.
Break out! Speak out! Cleanse and purify!
Be free of the shrouds that encase your life...
In your thoughts, your routine, your "rules."
Break those rules to grow to your own being.

TIME

Yesterday is gone; tomorrow has not yet come.
We have only today... we have only this second.
The advice that follows is, "Let us begin..."
The ball is in your court... you are expected to respond.

Time is an illusion; all we have is the present...
That little moment in time which we often miss, somehow.
The more you focus on time – past and future –
The more you miss the precious NOW!

You cannot buy time, but it is priceless.
You cannot own it; use it now with your knack.
You cannot keep it, but you can spend it;
And once it is lost, you can never get it back.

Time is like a river which keeps flowing on and on.
The flow that has passed will never pass again.
Don't waste your time in worries or regrets.
Life is too short to be unhappy. You don't need the pain.

Time moves in one direction, and memory in another.
Sometimes looking back becomes a favorite pastime.
Life is a one-time offer – don't waste it.
The trouble always is this: You think you have time.

WORDS

One word, wrongly spoken, can take on a life
Of its own, and you helplessly stand by
As it runs its course, whatever that is.
You see the devastation, and you cry.

Your words can be soft or kind as you speak,
Or they can be harsh as they enter the fray.
Season your words with tenderness, for
You may have to eat them some day.

Words have power to exalt or deplete.
They're more powerful than you think.
Your words are written on another's heart.
They're written in indelible ink.

Wrong words can spoil a meal or a snack,
Or whatever you have on your "plate."
We'd be better off if we worried more
About what we said than what we ate.

LIFE'S GIFTS

PERSEVERANCE

It is permanence, perseverance and persistence,
In spite of all obstacles thrown your way,
That takes you through to your destined place.
You accomplished it by pursuing it every day.
(Your struggle was worth it, I daresay.)

Patience and perseverance have a magical effect
Before which all obstacles disappear... they vanish.
Great works are performed not by strength alone,
But, it's by perseverance and persistence that you accomplish.
(Apply perseverance... you'll get your wish.)

You must have perseverance, and confidence in yourselves,
And believe that you are gifted for something.
Furthermore, believe this thing must be attained.
Pursue it, my loves. You have my blessing.
(You gain confidence from success, I am guessing.)

CONTINUUM

Each action that we think or do or say
Impacts those whom we meet along the way.
We trace our paths through life and find that we
Are linked with all that's in our galaxy.

We're part of what's gone on in years before,
Connected back beyond the "days of yore."
We're part of what is happening right now,
And must be mindful of what we endow.

For, action that we take while we're alive
Determines how the galaxy will survive.
It may be strange to think in terms like these...
But for today, be loving – will you please?

HEALTH

The first wealth is health! Did you hear this right?
I'll repeat it to make sure you heard the words.
THE FIRST WEALTH IS HEALTH – I meant to shout!
I wanted to make sure the words were heard.

Healthy body, healthy mind… they go hand in hand.
The mind follows the body as you trace your route.
Your duty is to keep your body at its peak
So that your mind can be clear as you walk about.

Good health and good sense are the two greatest blessings;
And, when we have them they become an expectation.
But when they're gone, you look back and ask the question:
Why, oh why, didn't I have more information
On how to live a healthier life?
Where did I go wrong in my calculation?

Time and health are two precious assets
That we don't appreciate or even recognize
Until they've been depleted. There's no getting them back!!
Why does it take so long to be wise?

Healthy food, healthy thoughts, and a positive attitude
Are the secrets to good health, and you can start now.
It's never too late to improve your lot in life!
With health you have hope; hope is everything somehow.

Good health is the thing that makes you feel
That now is the very best time of the year.
Let the natural forces within you keep you well.
Let your body take care of you, without fear.

ANGELS

The work of angels seems like sleight-of-hand magic.
We mostly believe only what our eyes see.
And since we don't usually expect to see angels,
They can do their work anonymously.

Angels are powerful spirits which are sent
By God to guide our way.
They work, without our seeing them,
For us when in work or play.

Pay attention the next time in conversation.
People use terms that let you know
That an angel has spread its wings over them
As they bask in the warm after-glow.

For example, when they say, "It was one of those days
That it felt good just to be alive,"
You can bet an angel had a part in their day;
A day for them to thrive.

Or how about, "I had a hunch
That everything would be okay for me."
Of course, an angel was there with the magic;
Their worries and fears were set free.

"I don't know where I ever found the courage..."
The sentence starts with awe in the voice.
The angels were watching, and when the time came –
Well, courage was their virtue of choice.

MEANING OF LIFE

Do you need a meaning in life
To achieve your happiness without any strife?
Most people feel a need to serve –
A vague notion, perhaps, but no plan in reserve.

There are some people who'll sublimate this urge
In business success – they are submerged
In doing the deal – in reading the bottom line,
But come up empty. It's hard to define.

Others seek fulfillment in political power,
Or wealth – or academics – the Ivory Tower?
All are secondary to the reason for living.
It's something different and, of course, involves giving.

It's "Live for God, love others, and be
A beacon to the world." It's a guarantee
To achieve the meaning of your being.
It's a simple concept, and one that is freeing.

HONOR

Honor is something you cannot win,
But it could be lost, I might remind.
Honor is not something that you take with you;
It is the heritage you leave behind.

You are never honored for what you receive.
Honor is the reward for what you give.
Those who give, hoping to be rewarded with honor,
Are not giving, but bargaining. (No way to live.)

Favor and honor sometimes fall more gracefully
On those who do not desire them, you see.
The greatest way to live with honor in this world
Is to make sure you are what you pretend to be.

At the end of the day, all you have is honor and trust.
Your reputation is built on trust and personal honor.
Show me the person(s) you honor the most
And I will know what kind of person you are.

WISDOM AND POWER

The wiser ones are those who know
That it is smartest to stay clear
Of a path of self-indulgence and
A pattern of self-centered fear.

Neurosis can appear to be thrilling
And fun with great excitement;
But leaves you tired and weak from wear.
It's behavior that is not intelligent.

Great power comes from being aware
Of what is going on around you;
And then acting upon that knowledge with
The purpose, the goal, of following through.

Your freedom comes from being obedient
To the Natural Order, a paradox?
Because, like it or not, it's the only way
To happiness. (Forgive the soapbox.)

Since all creation is one big whole,
Then feeling separate is an illusion.
Like it or not, we're on the same team.
Thinking otherwise leads to confusion.

Real power comes through cooperation.
Independence happens when you serve.
A greater self through selflessness
Emerges if you have the nerve.

SUFFERING

Hopefully, by the time you finish reading this poem,
You'll look at the subject of suffering
In a little different light, and maybe you'll welcome
Opportunity for character building without snuffling.

Character cannot be developed in peace and quiet –
Oh no, according to Helen Keller.
It's only through experience of trial and suffering
Can the soul be strengthened. (She's a hard–seller!)

"Out of suffering have emerged the strongest souls."
"The most massive characters are seared with scars."
So said Khalil Gibran who wrote *The Prophet.*
Take heart, his words are simply stellar!

All the world is full of suffering.
It's also full of overcoming one's dis–ease.
Man cannot remake himself without suffering,
For he's both the marble and sculptor, you see.

Tell your heart that the fear of suffering
Is worse than the suffering, it would seem.
And remember, no heart has ever suffered
When it goes in search of its dream.

Tennessee Williams did not mince words
When he spoke of suffering. And, he said,
"Don't look forward to the day you stop suffering,
Because when it comes, you'll know you are dead."

EXCITEMENT

Have you ever noticed that excitement and fear
Produce similar sensations – that you feel inside?
It's said that fear is just excitement in need
Of an attitude adjustment to be applied.

Besides, if something scares you, it might be the thing...
The very best thing... for you to be doing.
You will learn as you go; you'll meet the challenge,
And grow along the path you are pursuing.

The things that excite you are not random!
You'll find they're connected to your purpose.
So, follow them! Make them your life's work,
And your happiness and success will be glorious!

Excitement must lead to immediate action.
Don't lose the power of momentum.
Dreams can die if the moment for action passes.
Keep your life's regrets to a minimum!

Think of your life as an adventure.
Be excited to see where it takes you.
Let go of the fear and embrace the excitement,
As your dreams and ideas you pursue.

GIVING

The exchange of gifts has held us together
For more centuries than we can count.
When language struggles, a gift speaks volumes
To express feelings in various amounts.

If you came out a natural giver,
Your hands and heart were born open wide.
Though your hands might be empty with no 'things' to share
Your heart shares loving gifts, not to be denied.

A present is made for the pleasure of who gives it,
And not based on the merits of the recipient.
The reason is not important and should not be judged.
The gift is in the giving, you can be quite confident.

Giving to others liberates the soul of the giver,
Besides decreasing blood pressure and reducing stress.
It allows you to perceive others more positively.
You are happier as you 'pay it forward' to the rest.

A CLOSING THOUGHT

POETRY

It's the revelation
Of a sensation
That the poet
(Wouldn't you know it)
Believes to be
Felt only interiorly
And personal to
The writer who
... **writes it.**

It's the interpretation
Of a sensation
That was fueled by
A poet's sigh
And believed to be
Shared mutually
And personal to
The lucky one who
... **reads it.**

About the Author

Kathryn Carole Ellison is a former newspaper columnist
and journalist and, of course, a poet.

She lives near her children and stepchildren and their families in the
Pacific Northwest, and spends winters in the sunshine of Arizona.

You might find her on the golf course with friends, river rafting, traveling
the world, writing poems... or enjoying the Opera and the Symphony.

Late Bloomer

Our culture honors youth with all
It's unbridled effervescence.
We older ones sit back and nod
As if in acquiescence.

And when our confidence really gels
In early convalescence...
"We can't be getting old!" we cry,
"We're still struggling with adolescence!"

ACKNOWLEDGMENTS

I have many people to thank...

First of all, my amazing children—Jon and Nicole LaFollette—for inspiring the writing of these poems in the first place. And for encouraging me to continue my writing, even though their wisdom and compassion surpass mine... and to my dear daughter-in-law and friend, Eva LaFollette, whose encouragement and interest are so appreciated.

My wonderful stepchildren, Debbie and John Bacon, Jeff and Sandy Ellison, and Tom and Sue Ellison who, with their children and grandchildren, continue to be a major part of my life; and are loved deeply by me. These poems are for you, too.

My good friends who have received a poem or two of mine in their Christmas cards these many years, for complimenting me on the messages in my poems. Your encouragement kept me writing and gave me the courage to publish.

To Kim Kiyosaki who introduced me to the right person to get the publishing process under way... Mona Gambetta with Brisance Books Group. I marvel at her experience and know-how to make these books happen.

To Amy Anderson, Sonya Kopetz, Kerri Kazarba Schneider, and Ingrid Pape-Sheldon, my very creative public relations team of experts, who have carried my story to the world.

And finally, to John B. Laughlin, a fellow traveler in life, who encourages me every day in the writing and publishing process. John, I love having you in my cheering section.

BOOKS OF LOVE
by Kathryn Carole Ellison